Gideon's
BIBLE

Rick Salutin AND
Gideon Salutin

Gideon's
BIBLE

A Father & Son
Discuss God,
the Bible and Life

Illustrated by
Dušan Petričić

Foreword by
Margaret Atwood

Published by ECW Press
665 Gerrard Street East
Toronto, Ontario, Canada M4M 1Y2
416-694-3348 / info@ecwpress.com

Cover design: Dušan Petričić

LIBRARY AND ARCHIVES CANADA CATALOGUING IN PUBLICATION

Title: Gideon's bible / Rick Salutin and Gideon Salutin ; illustrated by Dušan Petričić ; foreword by Margaret Atwood.

Names: Salutin, Rick, author. | Salutin, Gideon, author. | Petričić, Dušan, illustrator. | Atwood, Margaret, 1939– writer of foreword.

Identifiers: Canadiana (print) 20200168746 | Canadiana (ebook) 20200168967
ISBN 9781770414853 (hardcover) | ISBN 9781773055213 (PDF)

Subjects: LCSH: Salutin, Rick. | LCSH: Salutin, Gideon. | LCSH: Bible—Appreciation. | LCSH: Bible.
Old Testament—Criticism, interpretation, etc., Jewish. | LCSH: Bible. New Testament—Criticism,
interpretation, etc., Jewish. | LCSH: Fathers and sons. | LCSH: Fathers and sons—Religious aspects—Judaism.

Classification: LCC BS538.5 .S25 2020 | DDC 220.6/1—dc23

The publication of *Gideon's Bible* has been generously supported by the Canada Council for the Arts which last year invested $153 million to
bring the arts to Canadians throughout the country and is funded in part by the Government of Canada. *Nous remercions le Conseil des arts du
Canada de son soutien. L'an dernier, le Conseil a investi 153 millions de dollars pour mettre de l'art dans la vie des Canadiennes et des Canadiens de tout le
pays. Ce livre est financé en partie par le gouvernement du Canada.* We acknowledge the support of the Ontario Arts Council (OAC), an agency of
the Government of Ontario, which last year funded 1,737 individual artists and 1,095 organizations in 223 communities across Ontario for a total
of $52.1 million. We also acknowledge the contribution of the Government of Ontario through Ontario Creates for the marketing of this book.

PRINTING: FRIESENS 5 4 3 2 1

PRINTED AND BOUND IN CANADA

To my teachers, Abraham Joshua Heschel and Nehama Leibowitz,
who masterfully combined the personal and the Biblical.

— Rick Salutin —

In memory of Ben Orenstein, and Passovers at the Holiday Inn.

— Gideon Salutin —

To my Dragana L. for all the years we spent together, and years we didn't spend.

— D.P. —

Your godmother says she'll write an introduction for us. It makes sense. She's known you since you were born.

And she's known you back to when you did all that religious stuff.

Margaret Atwood

first met Rick Salutin in 1958 at Camp White Pine, a liberal Jewish co-educational summer camp in Ontario. What was a nice not-Jewish girl like me doing there? Two things. It was an idealistic time — we believed in the brotherhood of man — so every summer, the camp director added several non-Jews to the staff. More prosaically, someone was needed to run the nature program, and who but myself would be willing to hang out in a converted tool shed preaching the virtues of toads, newts and mushrooms?

Rick was later to head up the Counsellor in Training unit, but at that moment he was visiting his co-conspirator at Holy Blossom Temple, Charles Pachter — not yet a leading artist, but a lowly arts and crafts assistant. Rick as a seventeen-year-old was in his ultra-religious phase. He was pious, superior, argumentative, judgmental and immersed in the Torah. I thought he was annoying, and he most likely thought I was an evil witch. Toad-whisperer I may have been, but Rick was on a first-name basis with God. Not that God has a second name.

Things changed several years later, when Rick gave up the idea of being a rabbi and took to writing. Now we could talk. It's a conversation that's been going on for over sixty years.

A large part of that conversation has been about his son, Gideon. BG Rick — Before Gideon Rick — couldn't really see the point of families, his own having been no shining example. But for Post-Gideon Rick, children were the most amazing thing — why didn't everyone have some? I became Gideon's godmother. Should

anything happen to not-always-healthy Rick, I'd be the safety net. I didn't undertake Gideon's moral education, however: Rick was doing that.

Or vice versa: nothing delighted Rick the Dad more than a snappy putdown of himself from his son. Gideon questioned everything, a trait he came by honestly. To witness the father-son dynamic in action was a lesson in the Socratic method, combined with Marxist dialectics and Biblical exegesis. When it came to the Bible, the two of them could go on for some time.

The sprightly but profound *Gideon's Bible* is the result of Gideon's questions as a child and then a teenager and Rick's attempts to answer them. It's partly a memoir, partly a father-son dialogue, albeit a somewhat unusual one. (Some dads just play baseball with their boys and leave it at that.) It showcases Rick's extensive knowledge of the Torah plus his refusal to tiptoe reverentially, as well as Gideon's insatiable curiosity plus his inherited bullshit meter.

It might also be called "The Biblical things you wanted to know but were too embarrassed to ask." What are the messages embedded in these ancient stories? Not always what you thought. The Bible has always been a Rorschach test of sorts: you get the Bible of your own fears and wishes.

The remarkable graphics by Dušan Petričić amplify both the Biblical stories and the ongoing modern story about a father and a son, extending the dynamic tradition of scriptural commentary that the book is modelled on.

Story-telling is arguably the most human of our human features. *Gideon's Bible* shows us that it's not just what you tell, it's how you tell it. And who you tell it for.

WHEN GIDEON WAS SMALL, HE ASKED:

Why did you give me this name?

HIS DAD, RICK, SAID,

It's from the Bible.

WHAT'S the BIBLE?

The Bible isn't really a book. It's a collection of books, like a one-volume box set. They were written over hundreds of years. Some weren't even written at first. They were passed on by word of mouth for generations before being recorded. The story starts with the creation of the world. Then it moves to the first humans, the first murder, a flood that nearly wipes everything out, and, pretty quickly, narrows down to the story of the Jewish people. Some books are just poems, prayers or thoughts, connected to that story. They're written in Hebrew. Afterward, Christians added stories about Jesus to the Hebrew Bible. So their Bible includes both. Later, Muslims based their holy book, the Quran, on Jewish and Christian Bibles.

WHEN RICK WAS YOUNG, HE OFTEN STUDIED THE BIBLE ALONG WITH HEBREW COMMENTARIES ON IT, ESPECIALLY ANCIENT ONES. HE ESPECIALLY ENJOYED COMMENTARIES PRINTED ON THE SAME PAGE AS THE BIBLICAL TEXT—WITH IT IN THE CENTRE AND COMMENTARIES FROM DIFFERENT AGES RUNNING DOWN THE SIDES OR ALONG THE TOP AND BOTTOM, ALL COMMENTING ON EACH OTHER. HE LIKED THE SENSE OF CONVERSATIONS ABOUT THE BIBLE THAT SEEMED TO BE HAPPENING ACROSS CENTURIES.

AS GIDEON GREW, HE AND RICK OFTEN DISCUSSED, AND THEN RE-DISCUSSED, MANY OF THOSE STORIES.

The Creation

When God began creating the sky and land, the land was shapeless and murky. There was darkness on the face of the deep, with God's spirit hovering over it. God said, Let there be light. And there was. God saw the light was good, and separated it from the darkness. He called the light Day and the darkness Night. So there was evening and morning: day one.

Then God said, Let there be a clear dome in the midst of the waters to separate those below it from those above. God called what was above the dome

Gideon and Rick visited Cape Spear in Newfoundland, the easternmost point in North America, one evening. The spray from waves bashing against rocks, along with mist, rain and clouds made any separation between water and sky indistinguishable. It was like a dense moist greyness, almost a curtain.

the Heavens, and there was evening and morning: day two. Then he said, Let the waters be drawn together so dry land appears. And it was so. Then he said, Let the earth sprout grass, plants, and fruit trees. That was so. Then he made two great lights: the largest to rule the day and the small one to preside over night, and the stars. Then God said, Let the waters swarm with life and let birds flutter upon earth and across the heavens. He also made great sea creatures and reptiles. He saw that was good so he blessed them, saying, Be fruitful and multiply. Then God said, Let the earth bring forth beasts of all kinds. And so it was, and he felt it was good.

Then you get leftwing and it pisses more people off. Then you piss off leftwing people because they think they're so holy and can never be wrong.

No. But yes.

No. Your timeline. First you get religious in high school to piss people like your parents off. Then you quit religion to piss religious people off.

Day one. God creates heaven and earth—

So let me get the timeline here.

What could I do, he had me cornered. I went to seminary. But I went to grad school at the same time.

What did you say?

He looked a bit like God. A lot of those guys I studied with did. He had a long beard. He even talked like God. He always had an answer. I once told him I didn't know if I wanted to go to the seminary because it seemed narrow and parochial. Not like a university, you know, the wide world of global learning. He said, 'My son,' you know, 'in the end' probably Moses was a very parochial man.

Tell me about Heschel in the meantime.

Gimme a minute to work this out—

Why do you think he made people?

GIDEON

RICK

Maybe so he wouldn't be lonely.

Or bored! And are they the same thing?

The Creation of human beings

Then God said, Let's make humans in our image, like us. And they'll rule over the fish in the sea, the birds in the sky, the animals everywhere on earth, and everything that wriggles along the ground. So God made them in his image, in his very own likeness, males and females, he created them. Then God blessed them, saying, Be fruitful and multiply. Fill the earth and control it. Rule over the fish in the sea, the birds in the sky, and all living things that move on the earth. He said, Look, I've given you all the plants with their seeds and the trees with their fruit for your food, and for the animals and birds, all the plants to eat. And so it was. God looked at everything he'd done and felt it was all very good. So there was evening and morning: day six. Then the heavens and earth were completed, and everything that goes with them. He finished on day seven, and rested, after everything he'd created and made.

There's an idea in Judaism that says before anything was created there was only God. God was everything. There was no time or space, just God. So for anything else to exist, God had to shrink himself. There's a Hebrew word for it. TSITMSTSOOM. It's one of those Jewish words that sounds like what it is.

Like KVETCH or SHLEP. Or OY VEY.

So, he did. God shrank himself. And in the tiny space he vacated, he put the whole world.

Because he was bored—

Or lonely. I had a teacher at the seminary. Abraham Joshua Heschel. Everyone called him Heschel. Even his wife. "Heschel," she said at a Passover seder, "Don't be so mystical." He wrote a book called God in Search of Man.

That's a cool title.

Heschel was cool. He marched with Martin Luther King Jr. for civil rights in the South in the U.S. In the 1960s.

So if God made people in his image, that shows he's human too.

Oh no. God in the Bible is completely different. He's all powerful, he's completely good and just. He knows everything.

But he gets lonely?

12

The Snake in the Garden

The snake was craftier than any other beast. He said to Eve, Did God tell you not to eat from any of the trees? She said, Not from the one in the middle of the garden, or we'll die. The snake said, You won't die. God knows when you eat from it your eyes will be opened and you'll be like God, knowing what's good and evil. So she took its fruit, ate, and gave some to Adam. Their eyes were opened and they knew they were naked. Then they heard God walking in the garden and hid. God said, Where are you? Adam said, I heard you and was afraid because I was naked. God said, Who told you that you're naked? Did you eat from that tree? Adam said, Eve made me. God said to her, What have you done? She said, The snake fooled me. God said to the snake, Because of this, you are cursed and on your belly you shall go. To Eve, he said, You'll give birth to your children in pain. And to Adam, Because you ate from that tree, from now on you'll work and sweat for your food. You'll return to the ground you came from. Dust you are and to dust you'll return. God thought, They've become like us, knowing good and evil. What if they also eat from the tree of life and live forever? So God drove them out of the garden.

Cain and Abel

Adam knew Eve. She became pregnant and had Cain, and then had his brother, Abel. Abel herded sheep while Cain farmed the ground. After a time, Cain brought the fruits of the earth as a gift for God. Meanwhile, Abel brought the best of his flock, and God preferred Abel's offering to Cain's. Cain was furious, his face fell. God said, Why this anger, why this look? If you do well, all will go well. But if not, bad things can happen—it's all up to you. Cain grumbled to Abel and then, in the field, he attacked and killed him. God said, Where's Abel, your brother? He said, I don't know, am I my brother's protector? God said: What have you done? Your brother's blood cries to me from the ground. Now you'll be cursed by the very earth that opened its mouth to take his blood from your hand. A wanderer and fugitive you'll be upon it. Cain said: This punishment is too great to bear. Look, you've driven me off the land and barred me from seeing your face. I'll wander and whoever finds me will kill me. God said, No. Anyone who strikes Cain will be struck back many times. Then God placed a mark on Cain, so none would harm him. Cain left and settled in the land of Nod, east of Eden. There he knew his wife, who had a son.

The Flood and the Rainbow

Coo.

I almost laughed.

Then it will be all right.

Martin Buber

Did he say anything?

YES—

He was quiet a long time. Then he asked if I had good friends. I said I thought so. He breathed out as if somebody lifted a weight off his chest.

Did he understand?

When I was a student in Jerusalem I went to see MARTIN BUBER, he was the wisest man I'd ever heard of. I told him about my sunsets.

That's kind of sad and kind of funny.

Exactly. As if life was in front of me but I couldn't reach it. I talked about it so much, my friends called it SALUTIN'S SUNSET.

Like the sun setting.

When I was in high school I worried my heart wouldn't leap up when I saw a rainbow or sunset. Especially sunsets. As soon as I saw one, I'd notice myself thinking, Look at me having this beautiful experience. Suddenly the experience would disappear behind the experience of having an experience.

Meh.

There's a poem I like: MY HEART LEAPS UP WHEN I BEHOLD A RAINBOW IN THE SKY.

What's so righteous about Noah? He doesn't try to warn people and save them. He just gets out with his family.

The commentaries say you can understand 'righteous in his time' in two ways. Either Noah was so good that EVEN in that awful era he was decent. Or—he was only good compared to the awful people around him.

God doesn't seem good either, why does he destroy them? Why doesn't he try to teach them, the way he did in the garden?

He promises not do it again.

That's like admitting he shouldn't have done it at all. He doesn't even say he won't do it again, just: not WITH A FLOOD. It's like he sort of coughs and says behind his hand: by water that is.

God saw the evil done by men was great, and regretted placing them on earth. He said, I'll wipe them from the earth, not just them but beasts, reptiles, and birds. But Noah found favour in God's eyes. He was a righteous, innocent man in his time. So God said to him, Make yourself a wooden ark. Then I'll bring a flood onto the earth to wipe out all flesh. But I'll make an agreement with you. Enter the ark, you, your sons, your wife, and your sons' wives. And from all living things, bring two of each kind. Seven days later the flood came. The fountains of the deep burst, the windows of the heavens opened. It rained forty days and forty nights. All flesh perished. Only Noah remained, and those with him. Then God remembered Noah, so he sent a wind and the waters withdrew. The ark came to rest on the mountains of Ararat. God said to Noah and his children, Look, I've made an agreement that never again will all flesh be wiped out by a flood. This is the sign I give you: my rainbow in the clouds. So, whenever there are clouds over the earth, the rainbow will appear, and I'll recall it.

If he's the only god in the Bible, why does he say, Let's go down there. He's talking to somebody.

It could be the royal we.

That's feeble. Maybe it's angels. Or lesser gods. Or his heavenly court.

Even if that's true—just for the sake of argument—he still doesn't seem to care much about them. In other mythologies, like Greek or Hindu, the gods are obsessed with each other: they play, love, fight, plot. Humans are just toys and distractions.

That's true. Greek gods treat the Trojan War like entertainment. They mess with people if they're bored with gods.

The Tower of Babel

Turm von Babylon

BABEL-TORONY KINEK

Πύργος της Βαβέλ

Вавилонская башня

Torre de Babel

TOREN VAN BABEL

BABEL

BABIL KULESI

Tour de Babel

TORRE DI BABELE

Just kidding. It's the Jewish people, right?

Er, sort of.

A focus group?

A group actually.

Who's the lucky victim?

Funny—that's more or less what he does.

Then he should stay away. Hang out with other gods or whatever they are. Take a parenting course. Maybe find somebody to practise on.

Maybe it's not easy to deal with humans if you're God.

Before the flood, things were simple. There were few people. After, everything expands, there are groups, but they all speak one language—it's idyllic. They could've done anything if they stuck together. It's as if everything started going too well and God got scared of their power. But that's paranoid—they aren't defying him. Why isn't he proud, like a parent? He made them—he gave them the ability to disobey. Then he throws a fit—like a child. He didn't destroy the whole world, but he wiped out a great civilization.

At that time the whole earth had one language with a common vocabulary. As people migrated from the east, they discovered a plain in the land of Shinar and settled there. They said to each other, Now let's make bricks, and bake them till they're hard. They used the bricks as if they were stones, and tar as mortar. Then they said, All right, now let's build ourselves a city with a tower that has its top in the heavens, and make ourselves famous, instead of just continuing to disperse across the face of the earth. God descended to see this city with its tower, that these descendants of Adam had built, and he thought, Hmm, they've become one people with one language between them, and this is just the start of what they might do. What would be beyond them if they dare to attempt it? Let's go down there and scramble their language, so none can comprehend his neighbours' speech. So he scattered them from there across the face of the earth and they never finished their city. That's why it was called Babel: because it was there that God muddled their speech and spread them all over the earth.

In the Bible, even hints like Let's Go Down There are rare. Mostly, other divine beings don't appear. Or fade from view. God focusses on people.

Like what?

That's a pretty surprising choice if you're God. I'm impressed. But if he's so focussed on people, why doesn't he do a better job with them?

Abraham gets out

God said to Abram, Get yourself out of your country, your birthplace, and your father's house to a land I'll show you. I'll make you into a great nation. I'll bless those who bless you, and whoever curses you, I'll curse. Through you all the earth's peoples will be blessed. So Abram went, as God commanded. He was seventy-five. He took Sarai his wife, Lot his nephew, all their goods and servants, and headed for Canaan. Canaanites lived there then. God appeared again, saying, I'll give this land to your descendants. But there was a famine. So Abram went down to Egypt to stay there. When they neared Egypt, he said to Sarai, Look, you're a beautiful woman and when the Egyptians see you, they'll say, She's his wife. Then they'll kill me and let you live. Please say you're my sister, so all goes well and my life is spared. When Pharaoh's princes saw her, they praised her to him and she was taken to his palace. Because of her he dealt well with Abram. But God struck Pharaoh and his household with great plagues because of Sarai. Pharaoh summoned Abram and said, What's this? Why didn't you say she's your wife? Why did you say she's your sister? Take her and get out. So Pharaoh's men sent them all away.

After Abraham gets out

That night, Rick thinks about their conversations. Rick is no longer religious, but his ideas on the Bible are still rooted in what he learned in synagogue school or the seminary. For instance, that the God of the Bible is almighty, all-knowing, just, good, and perfect. When you're taught a certain way, it's hard not to keep thinking that way when you're older.

Gideon comes at it differently. He wasn't raised in a religious tradition, so he doesn't see it through anyone else's eyes. He goes straight to it. For him, God in the Bible is a bit of a dick and a bit of a spoiled brat. He's powerful but not all-powerful.

Rick has to admit that may really be how God is in the Bible, versus how Rick was taught. Traits like perfection and omnipotence might've been added later, by rabbis and interpreters, even if they weren't in the actual text. In fact, if you look at the Bible itself, God isn't all-knowing, just, or perfect—though he has his good moments. It's amazing how differently you see the character called God (who has a name just as Greek gods like Zeus do) if you don't view him through a later tradition. Since Gideon comes to the Bible directly, in a way Rick can't, he has a valuable ability to see things in his own, unique way.

These disagreements where Gideon turns out to be right are a long tradition between them.

18

Abraham's first son

It's so human. First she says take Hagar, then she's jealous.

What's with 'H' replacing 'I'?

It's from God's name. H is part of it.

What's the name?

This is weird, I'm trying not to say it. Religious Jews never did, out of respect or fear or superstition. They used euphemisms. They said 'The Name.' OK. or 'The Name'. OK. It's YHVH. No one knows how it was spoken. Vowels don't show in Biblical Hebrew, so you guess. Maybe 'Yahveh'.

Are you worried you'll be hit by lightning now?

Don't be a smartass. Some habits stick. You didn't even know they were still there.

What happens to Ishmael?

He becomes father of the Arabs. Isaac's the son who inherits God's promises to Abraham. He's younger.

Did Ishmael lose out because he's only half-Jewish like me?

Partly. Also because he's the firstborn.

I thought that was a plus, like being crown prince.

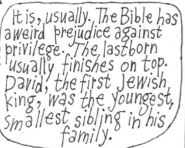

It is, usually. The Bible has a weird prejudice against privilege. The lastborn usually finishes on top. David, the first Jewish king, was the youngest, smallest sibling in his family.

S arai had given Abram no children. She had an Egyptian servant named Hagar. She said, Look, God has stopped me from having children. So take my servant; maybe I'll be renewed through her. Abram agreed. So Sarai gave Hagar to him as a wife. He came to her and she conceived. At that, her mistress diminished in her eyes. Then Sarai said to Abram, It's your fault. I sent her into your arms. Now she's pregnant and disrespects me. Let God judge. Abram answered, She's yours; do what seems best. So Sarai punished her and she fled. A messenger from God found her by a spring in the desert and said, Where are you from and where are you going? She said, I am fleeing my mistress. He said, Return and debase yourself before her. You will have a son. Call him Ishmael, for God has heard your sorrow. His descendants will be too many to count. He'll be a beast of a man, in conflict with everyone. So Hagar bore Abram a son, Ishmael. God said, Sarai's name shall now be Sarah. I'll bless her, and give you another son through her. Abraham fell down laughing, thinking, Will a hundred-year-old man have a child? Will Sarah, who's ninety?

Like the Bible. It embraces the underdogs. Sweet.

The vet said he might not make it. But you picked him anyway.

GIDEON'S CAT He was rescued from the streets and Gideon chose him over other available kittens.

Like Keiko. He was a runt when we got him.

The underdog's the favourite? Why?

It doesn't say. But Abraham's people were latecomers.

Weird. They seem so ancient. Aren't Jews 'The Eternal People'?

Not back then. Egypt was mighty long before. Abraham left a great civilization where Iraq is now. The first Jews had an underdog experience.

Abraham and His Visitors

God appeared as Abraham sat by the tent opening in the heat of the day. He lifted his eyes and saw three men. He ran and said, My lords, if I find favour in your eyes, don't pass; let water be brought to wash your feet and relax, while I bring food. He set it out and stood under the tree as they ate. They said, Where's Sarah, your wife? He answered, In the tent. Then one said, I'll return at this time next year, and she'll have a son. Sarah was listening behind the flap. She laughed to herself, When I'm worn out and no desire's left in me? God said, Why did she laugh? Is any wonder beyond God? Sarah was afraid and said, I didn't. He said, Oh, yes, you did.

So the three guys are God, or the other two are his crew?

Search me. The one who talks must be God.

It's nice that she laughs. There aren't lots of laughs in the Bible.

Or we miss them because it's so 'holy'?

Like writing essays on Great Authors for courses. It's so serious.

Kafka and Joyce are actually hilarious. They cracked up their friends. So's your godmother* But it can get lost in all the reverence for 'literature'.

* See Foreword

20

Sodom and Gomorrah

↓1

Abraham says, Great. But, er, one more thing. Would you really waste them if–? God is like, Fine, OK– He's probably cracking up by then. Abraham has such nerve. What do you call that in Yiddish– –Chutzpah?

Yah.

How would you translate it?

CHUTZPAH.

They're like a couple of guys dicking around. Except one is God.

It has an intimacy you don't often see between gods and humans. Pious people sometimes find it offensive.

It's like Groucho and Chico. You told me these stories were performed.

Probably. At solemn feasts after the harvest or holy days like Yom Kippur.

God's Groucho and Abe's Chico.

BY THE TIME HE WAS 10, GIDEON HAD MEMORIZED MANY SCENES FROM MARX BROTHERS MOVIES.

Then the men rose, heading toward Sodom. Abraham went along to see them off. God thought, Should I hide from him what I'm going to do? I've come to know him, I'm sure he'll tell his descendants to follow my ways and do the right thing. So God said, The outcry of Sodom and Gomorrah is loud and their sin is great. I'll go there now and see, to be sure. The others headed off but Abraham remained before God. He said, Will you really sweep away the just with the wicked? Suppose there are 50 just people there. Won't you save it for their sake? It's not like you to kill the just with the wicked. Will the judge of all the earth not act justly? God said, Fine. If I find 50, I'll spare it. Abraham went on, Now I've dared speak—and I'm mere dust and ashes. But maybe 5 out of 50 will be absent. Would you slaughter a city over 5? He said, No, not if I find 45. He persisted, Maybe only 40 will be found. He said, For 40 I won't. Then he said, Please don't be angry, but how about 30? He said, Not if I find 30. He said, Now I'm going too far. But if there are 20? He said, Not for 20. Then he said, Please don't be angry, one last time: if there are 10? He said, I won't do it. So God left, and Abraham returned to his place.

A DAY AT THE RACES

No it's not that book. You haven't got that book.

TIPS ON BETTING ON HORSES

You've got it huh? I'll get it in a minute though won't I? How much is it?

One dollar.

And it's the last book I'm buying.

ICE CREAM

↓2

What happened when they got to the cities?

Sodom and Gomorrah didn't make it. They were too violent. They tried to force the visitors to have sex with them.

There's a lot of sex in this book.

The only good people were Abraham's nephew Lot and his family. They protected the visitors. So they escaped the destruction.

Not from a flood I hope.

Fireballs raining from the heavens this time.

But they got away.

Except Lot's wife. They were told not to look back but she did and turned into a pillar of salt.

I suppose there's a lesson there: Don't look back?

Something might be gaining on you.

Who said that?

SATCHEL PAIGE. GREAT BLACK BASEBALL PLAYER BORN 1906. CAME TO THE MAJORS RIGHT AFTER JACKIE ROBINSON. I SAW HIM PITCH IN TORONTO. HE WAS 51.

My dad, the Heritage Minute.

21

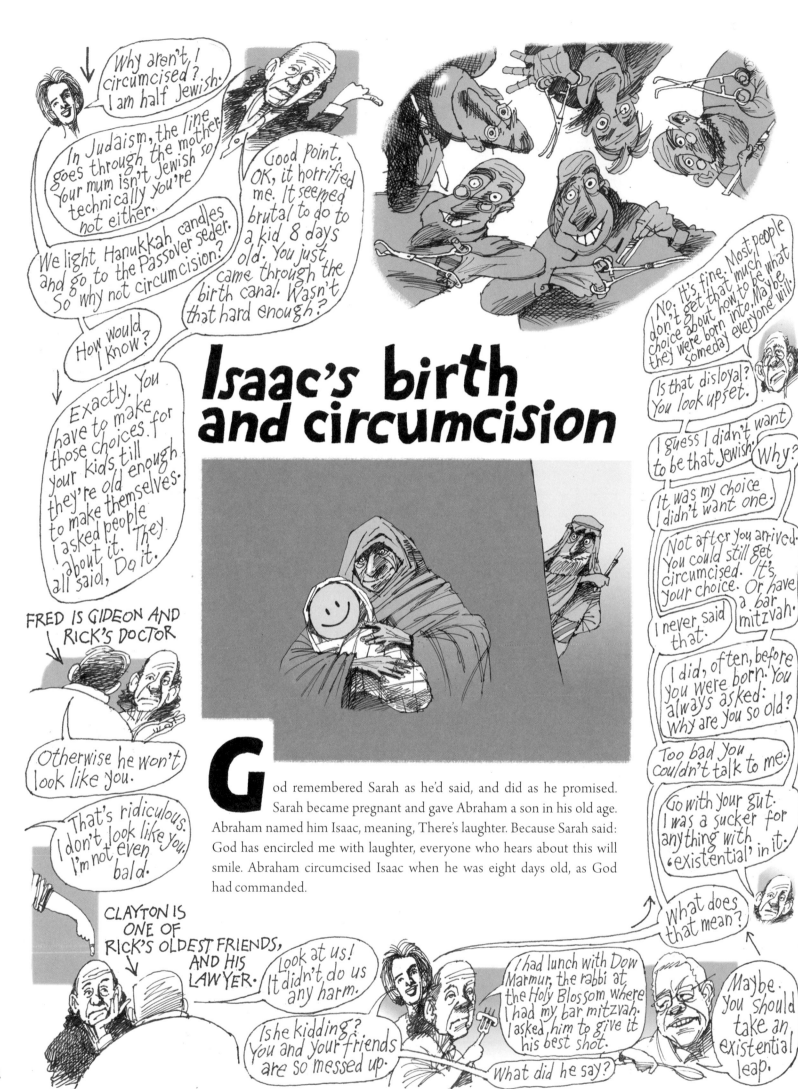

Isaac's birth and circumcision

Why aren't I circumcised? I am half Jewish.

In Judaism, the line goes through the mother. Your mum isn't Jewish so technically you're not either.

We light Hanukkah candles and go to the Passover seder. So why not circumcision?

Good point. OK, it horrified me. It seemed brutal to do to a kid 8 days old. You just came through the birth canal. Wasn't that hard enough?

How would I know?

Exactly. You have to make those choices for your kids till they're old enough to make themselves. I asked people about it. They all said, Do it.

FRED IS GIDEON AND RICK'S DOCTOR

Otherwise he won't look like you.

That's ridiculous. I don't look like you. I'm not even bald.

CLAYTON IS ONE OF RICK'S OLDEST FRIENDS, AND HIS LAWYER.

Look at us! It didn't do us any harm.

Is he kidding? You and your friends are so messed up.

God remembered Sarah as he'd said, and did as he promised. Sarah became pregnant and gave Abraham a son in his old age. Abraham named him Isaac, meaning, There's laughter. Because Sarah said: God has encircled me with laughter, everyone who hears about this will smile. Abraham circumcised Isaac when he was eight days old, as God had commanded.

No. It's fine. Most people don't get that much choice about how to be what they were born into. Maybe someday everyone will.

Is that disloyal? You look upset.

I guess I didn't want to be that Jewish. Why?

It was my choice. I didn't want one.

Not after you arrived. You could still get circumcised. It's your choice. Or have a bar mitzvah.

I never said that.

I did, often, before you were born. You always asked: Why are you so old?

Too bad you couldn't talk to me.

Go with your gut. I was a sucker for anything with 'existential' in it.

What does that mean?

I had lunch with Dow Marmur, the rabbi at the Holy Blossom where I had my bar mitzvah. I asked him to give it his best shot.

What did he say?

Maybe you should take an existential leap.

22

Abraham's test

This story got me interested in the Bible.

Did I tell you it?

No. It was Dylan's song.

God said to Abraham, Kill me a son. Abe said, Man you must be puttin me on... God said, You can do what you want Abe but, next time you see me comin', you better run. Abe said, Where you want this killin' done?

The story in the Bible's so skimpy. Just DUM, DUM, DUM.

Drumbeats on the way to a hanging.

Dylan gives you more, though he leaves lots out too.

T

hen God tested Abraham: Abraham! Yes?

Take your son, *your only son,* who you love—

Isaac, and offer him as a sacrifice on a hill I'll show you. Abraham rose next day, saddled his donkey, took two young men, and Isaac. He cut wood for a sacrifice and went where God indicated. Three days later, he saw it. He told the men, Stay with the donkey. I and the lad will pray and return. He loaded the wood onto Isaac, took the flint and knife himself, and off they went. Isaac said, Father . . . Yes? said Abraham. I see the flint and wood but where's the lamb to sacrifice? Abraham said, God will provide it, my boy. They arrived and Abraham built an altar. He laid out the wood, bound Isaac, and placed him on it. Then Abraham raised the knife to slaughter him. But a messenger of God called, Abraham! He said, I'm here. He said, Don't strike the boy or harm him, for I can see that you tremble before God. Abraham looked up and saw a ram caught in a thicket. He sacrificed it instead. The messenger called again: Because you've done this, not sparing your son, God will bless you and multiply your offspring like the stars above and the sand on the shore. Through them, all peoples will be blessed. Then Abraham returned to his men. They all rose and went together.

They aren't Groucho and Chico here.

Imagine Isaac looking up at the look on Abraham's face.

It's the terrifying side of God. The poet Blake called it Tyger, Tyger, burning bright, in the forests of the night.

He sounds like Dylan.

This passage was my bar mitzvah reading. Weirdly, on the Saturday after you were born, someone from the synagogue up the street knocked and asked me to join their service. They never had before.

THE SHUL AT THE CORNER

↓

I left your mum and tiny you in the livingroom. When I got there, this was part of that week's Torah portion. It starts with Abraham learning he'll have a son when he's old and ends with almost killing Isaac. I looked over the shoulder of the cantor reading the same words I spoke when I turned 13. It was spooky.

Tyger, Tyger.

Isaac meets Rebekah

After Sarah's death, Abraham told his servant: Go to my family's homeland and find Isaac a wife. The servant took ten camels and went. He had them kneel by a well in the evening, when Rebekah appeared with a pitcher on her shoulder. She said she was Abraham's brother's granddaughter and invited him to stay with them. They laid food before him but he said, I won't eat till I explain my purpose. I'm Abraham's servant and God has led me here to bring my master's brother's granddaughter for his son.

They said, This thing's from God, what can we say? Take her. They ate, drank, and slept. Next morning, he said, Now send us back. But her brother and mother said, Let her stay a few days. Don't delay me, he replied. They answered, Let's get her opinion. They called Rebekah and asked, Will you go with him? She said, I will. So they sent her and her servant . . .

Isaac went into the fields at sunset to think, looked up, and saw camels approaching. Rebekah looked up too, saw Isaac, and dismounted. The servant told him everything. Isaac brought her into Sarah's tent and she became his wife. He loved her and felt comforted for his mother's loss . . .

Abraham breathed his last and died at a good old age. Isaac and Ishmael buried him in the cave of Machpelah, alongside Sarah.

Why doesn't Isaac go?

It's not how things were done.

OK, but still...

Yah. You're right. There's something passive about him.

Like going into the field — just to think?

I wonder what he thought about.

What else: the thing his father almost did. He'll think about that the rest of his life. With no answer. Because there isn't one. Even Rebekah's more assertive. I was surprised when she said she'd leave.

If they'd expected that, they probably wouldn't have asked.

Maybe Isaac misses his mother so much because she didn't try to kill him.

I also wonder what it did to Abraham — though he became the father of his people because of it. He's called Abraham Our Father. Even Moses is just Moses Our Teacher.

You know, in the end, Ishmael may have got the better deal.

Sarah sent Ishmael and his mother away again after Isaac's birth.

I'm glad Ishmael's there for Abraham's burial. It's weird that God called Isaac "your only son" when he ordered Abraham to sacrifice him.

Nelson Mandela had a botched relationship with his kids too, because he was in prison while they grew up. He said, "To be the father of a nation is a great honour. But to be the father of a family is a great joy." He never had that joy.

The birth of twins

Isaac appealed to God on Rebekah's behalf, since she was childless. God responded and she became pregnant. But the children battled inside her and she said, If this is how it's going to be, what's the point? She went to ask God and he said, Two nations are inside you and will be separated there. The older will serve the younger.

When the time arrived, out came the twins. The first was reddish, as if he had a hairy cloak, so they called him Esau. Then his brother emerged, his hand clutching Esau's heel, so they called him Jacob. When they grew up, Esau was a skilled hunter, a man of the fields. Jacob was simpler, a dweller in tents. Isaac loved Esau—for the food he brought—but Rebekah loved Jacob. Once when Jacob was cooking, Esau returned from hunting, worn out, and said, Give me some of that red stew, I'm exhausted! First sell me your inheritance, said Jacob. Esau said, I'm dying here, what good's an inheritance? Promise it then, said Jacob. Right now. Esau did, and Jacob gave him bread with stew. He ate and drank and rose and left. So Esau scorned his birthright.

She 'went to ask God.' Does that mean she prayed?

Or actually went somewhere, like a shrine, and paid someone to ask God things.

Like a Greek oracle.

Maybe. Everyone then probably knew what it meant.

What's with the names.

Jacob has 'heel' in it. Esau comes from hair.

He hung onto his brother's heel. You can see what he's like as soon as he's out. Determined.

We could tell what you were like too. The nurse didn't put eyedrops in right away, so you could see clearly. You lay on your mom's chest and looked around and around. You were already an observer. A student.

If the older serves the younger—what about Christians or Muslims? They came after Jews. Do they think they should take over from Jews?

Early Christians did. Maybe they got the idea from stories like this. We're here now, they said. You Jews should join us. Jesus said the first will be last and the last will be first.

It's kind of revolutionary. Nobody's secure in their privilege.

Another brother story.

The Bible's a master class in sibling rivalry. Freud feasted on them.

He was Jewish, right?

Very. He wrote a book debunking Moses and Judaism. He also had a bust of Moses in his office. It was classic Freudian, and Jewish, ambivalence.

Moses watched him and he watched his patients. I like it.

Jacob deceives Isaac

When Isaac was old and his eyes dim, he said to Esau, I'm old, I don't know when I'll die. Get your bow. Hunt game, cook it as I like, and I'll bless you before I die. Rebekah was listening. When Esau left, she told Jacob, Do what I say. Bring two lambs. I'll make them the way your father loves. Then take them to him, so he blesses you instead. Jacob said, But Esau's hairy and I'm smooth. What if father feels me and knows I'm lying? She said, Just do it. She found Esau's clothes and put them on Jacob. She laid skins of goats on his hands and neck. He went to Isaac. Father . . . Who are you? I'm Esau. Come, eat, and bless me. Isaac said, How did you get back so quickly? Approach, so I can feel you. Jacob did. Isaac felt him and said, The voice is Jacob's, but the hands are Esau's. He blessed him but added:

Jacob becomes the third 'father' of his people, after Abraham and Isaac.

HE'S A CROOK. NOT A HERO.

All heroes aren't heroic. Odysseus was a wily schemer who outlasted other Greek heroes.

He cheats his brother–twice. And fools his dad. He's a liar!

Er, lying isn't always bad.

Is lying good?

Listen, when you were 5, we went to LEGOLAND in England.

I remember, it was great.

You wanted to drive the bumper cars but the sign said you had to be 6. They asked how old you were so I said, 6. They let us in. You said—!

So you have to learn to be a 'good' liar—and a good liar?

If it does good and not harm. It's tricky.

That lying is OK?

I think you knew adults don't always tell the truth themselves but tell their kids not to lie. Maybe this helped you understand.

I wonder what I meant.

Is that really you? As soon as Jacob left, Esau arrived and said, Eat, father, and bless me. Isaac said, Who are you? He said, Esau. Isaac shuddered and said, Then who was here earlier? I blessed him, and now it's gone? Esau cried a hoarse bitter cry: Bless me too! But Isaac said, Your brother fooled me and stole it. Esau said, He's displaced me twice: first my birthright, now my blessing.

Daddy, YOU LIED.

Yes, lying isn't always bad. Especially if no one gets hurt and something good comes from it. I know you really want to drive that car.

You drove brilliantly. As you were falling asleep that night, you said—

Daddy, I liked it when you lied.

Jacob's flight and his dream

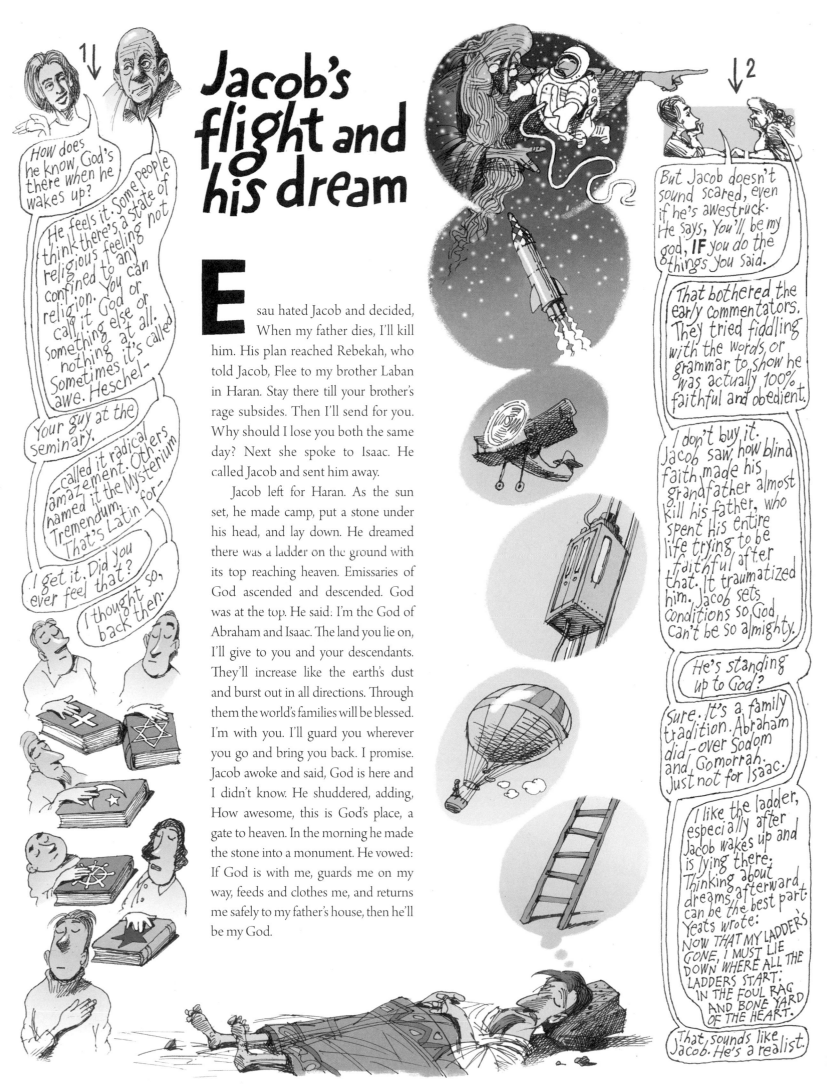

How does he know God's there when he wakes up?

He feels it. Some people think there's a state of religious feeling not confined to any religion. You can call it God or something else or nothing at all. Sometimes it's called awe. Heschel—

Your guy at the seminary.

—called it radical amazement. Others named it the Mysterium Tremendum. That's Latin for—

I get it. Did you ever feel that?

I thought so, back then.

Esau hated Jacob and decided, When my father dies, I'll kill him. His plan reached Rebekah, who told Jacob, Flee to my brother Laban in Haran. Stay there till your brother's rage subsides. Then I'll send for you. Why should I lose you both the same day? Next she spoke to Isaac. He called Jacob and sent him away.

Jacob left for Haran. As the sun set, he made camp, put a stone under his head, and lay down. He dreamed there was a ladder on the ground with its top reaching heaven. Emissaries of God ascended and descended. God was at the top. He said: I'm the God of Abraham and Isaac. The land you lie on, I'll give to you and your descendants. They'll increase like the earth's dust and burst out in all directions. Through them the world's families will be blessed. I'm with you. I'll guard you wherever you go and bring you back. I promise. Jacob awoke and said, God is here and I didn't know. He shuddered, adding, How awesome, this is God's place, a gate to heaven. In the morning he made the stone into a monument. He vowed: If God is with me, guards me on my way, feeds and clothes me, and returns me safely to my father's house, then he'll be my God.

But Jacob doesn't sound scared, even if he's awestruck. He says, You'll be my god, **IF** you do the things you said.

That bothered the early commentators. They tried fiddling with the words, or grammar, to show he was actually 100% faithful and obedient.

I don't buy it. Jacob saw how blind faith made his grandfather almost kill his father, who spent his entire life trying to be faithful after that. It traumatized him. Jacob sets conditions so God can't be so almighty.

He's standing up to God?

Sure. It's a family tradition. Abraham did—over Sodom and Gomorrah. Just not for Isaac.

I like the ladder, especially after Jacob wakes up and is lying there. Thinking about dreams afterward can be the best part. Yeats wrote: NOW THAT MY LADDER'S GONE, I MUST LIE DOWN WHERE ALL THE LADDERS START: IN THE FOUL RAG AND BONE YARD OF THE HEART.

That sounds like Jacob. He's a realist.

27

Jacob meets Rachel

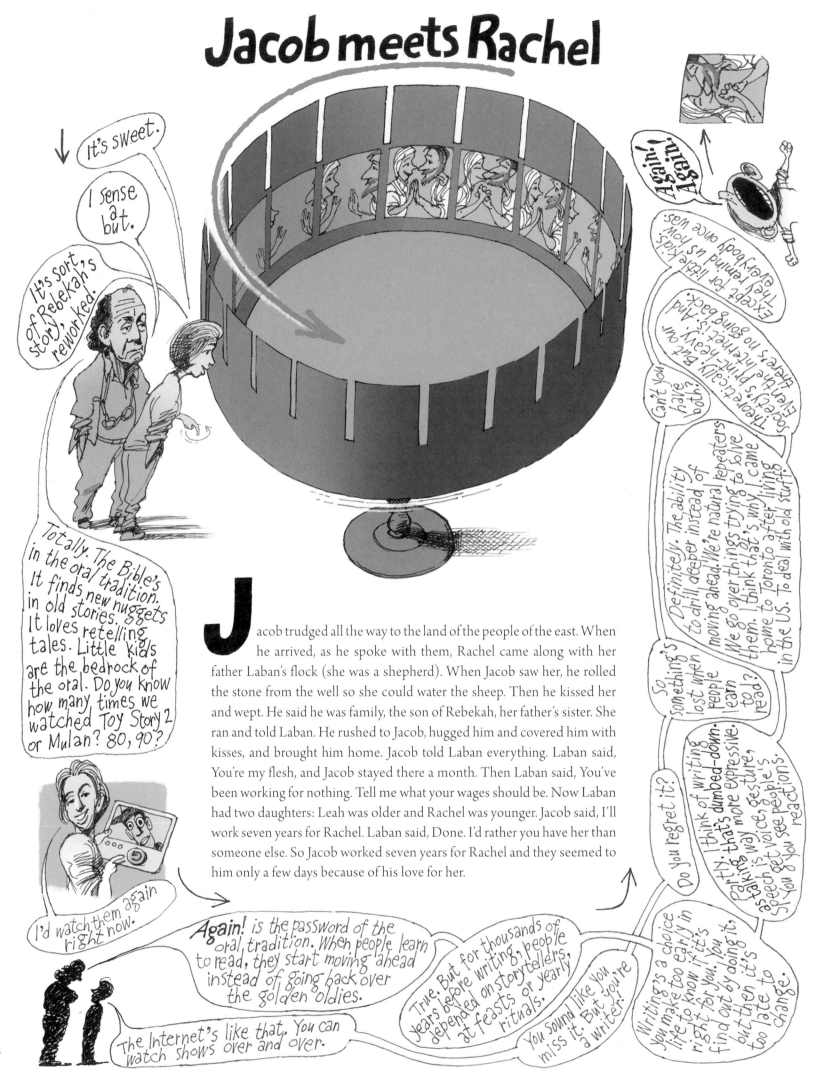

It's sweet.

I sense a but.

It's sort of Rebekah's story, reworked!

Totally. The Bible's in the oral tradition. It finds new nuggets in old stories. It loves retelling tales. Little kids are the bedrock of the oral. Do you know how many times we watched Toy Story 2 or Mulan? 80, 90?

I'd watch them again right now.

Again! Again!

Except for little kids. They remind us how everybody once was.

Theoretically, sure. But our society's print-heavy. And there's no going back.

Can't you have both?

Definitely. The ability to drill deeper instead of moving ahead. We're natural repeaters. We go over things trying to solve them. I think that's why I came home to Toronto after living in the US. To deal with old stuff.

So something's lost when people learn to read?

I think of writing partly as dumbed-down. Talking is a way more expressive, gesture, speech get peoples' reactions. You get to see peoples' reactions.

Do you regret it?

Writing's a choice you make too early in life to know if it's right for you. You find out by doing it, but then it's too late to change.

You sound like you miss it. But you're a writer!

True. But for thousands of years before writing, people depended on storytellers, at feasts or yearly rituals.

Again! is the password of the oral tradition. When people learn to read, they start moving ahead instead of going back over the golden oldies.

The Internet's like that. You can watch shows over and over.

Jacob trudged all the way to the land of the people of the east. When he arrived, as he spoke with them, Rachel came along with her father Laban's flock (she was a shepherd). When Jacob saw her, he rolled the stone from the well so she could water the sheep. Then he kissed her and wept. He said he was family, the son of Rebekah, her father's sister. She ran and told Laban. He rushed to Jacob, hugged him and covered him with kisses, and brought him home. Jacob told Laban everything. Laban said, You're my flesh, and Jacob stayed there a month. Then Laban said, You've been working for nothing. Tell me what your wages should be. Now Laban had two daughters: Leah was older and Rachel was younger. Jacob said, I'll work seven years for Rachel. Laban said, Done. I'd rather you have her than someone else. So Jacob worked seven years for Rachel and they seemed to him only a few days because of his love for her.

Jacob's wedding night

Jacob stole his blessing. But he still has to earn it.

How does that work here?

THE ARC OF HISTORY IS LONG BUT IT BENDS TOWARD JUSTICE.

Those things still puzzle me but I think I agree with Martin Luther King.

I knew we had to go to Sherwood Forest. So we did.

ARE BAD GUYS NICE TO EACH OTHER?

In your carseat you once asked me:

It was about good guys and bad guys!

You've always been fascinated by moral issues. It's why you loved Robin Hood.

Jacob said, I've completed my time. Now give me my wife and I'll be with her. So Laban gathered the local people and held a feast. In the evening he took Leah and brought her to Jacob, who went in with her. In the morning, he saw it was Leah! He said to Laban, What's this you've done? You know I worked for Rachel. Why have you deceived me? Laban said, We don't do things that way here—giving the younger before the first-born. Finish the week with this one and you'll get the other too. If you work for me another seven years, that is. So Jacob did. He finished the week and got Rachel as a wife. He went to her and loved her more than Leah—and then he worked for Laban seven more years.

It's like Laban's taunting Jacob. He says, We've heard how you do things over there in Canaan. But you're not in Canaan now.

Laban must've made sure Jacob was drunk, then he switched Leah for Rachel. He probably sized Jacob up right away. He didn't arrive on 10 camels with gifts. He was in a weak bargaining position.

But Jacob deserved it even if Laban cheated him. Because he cheated his own brother. And lied to his father.

So it's moral payback. The evil you do is done to you.

It's very symmetrical. Jacob fools Isaac because he can't see. Then Laban fools Jacob because it's dark and he's drunk and **he** can't see.

It's almost like Laban's really talking about Esau. He doesn't say, 'We don't give the younger before the older.' He says 'before the firstborn.'

But I see Jacob's point too. Just because he was born second, he didn't get a birthright or a blessing so he had a right to cheat a bit to even it up.

29

The battle of the babies

Jacob's being a jerk here. He barks at Rachel and he's mean to Leah. Then God comes along. We haven't seen him for a while. Unlike Jacob, he notices their distress and treats them with kindness. Good for God.

He's a mensch.

Yeah, he's a bro.

Did you ever feel desperate about not having kids? Rachel says it's like death.

I wanted it for decades. I'd pretty much given up. I wrote a book where a character asks himself: Can you justify a childless life?

Did he have an answer?

The answer was: It's better not to have to.

But you CAN justify it.

OF COURSE.

I'M JUST GLAD...

...I DIDN'T...

...HAVE TO.

This part about the knees is like THE HANDMAID'S TALE. We read it in English class. It's in the tv series too. Do you think the idea came from here?

Lots of stuff from the Bible shows up in books. People use its language all the time, sometimes they don't even know where it's from.

Like using lines from Shakespeare in daily life.

Exactly. And guess where Shakespeare got a lot of those.

They had 11 sons and only one daughter? Not very likely.

They probably didn't mention the girls. Unless there's a reason, like Dinah. She comes up later. The Bible's economical that way.

Yah. And misogynistic. Joseph's born last. We know what that means by now. He's gonna be a player, right? The last is first.

When God saw Leah was hated, he opened her womb, but Rachel was childless. Leah had a son, who she called Reuben, thinking, Now my husband will love me. Then she had another, Simon, then Levi, and then Judah. Then she stopped. When Rachel saw those children, she envied Leah. She said, Give me children too or I'm dead. It angered Jacob. He said, What? Am I God, who can block your birth canal? So she said, Here's my maid Bilhah; come to her, she'll give birth onto my knees and I'll be renewed through her. Bilhah conceived and gave Jacob a son who Rachel called Dan. Then a second, Naftali. When Leah saw she'd stopped giving birth, she gave her servant Zilpah to Jacob. She gave him a son, Gad, and another, Asher. Then Reuben, Leah's first, went out during the harvest and found aphrodisiac plants. He gave them to his mother. Rachel said, Let me have those, please. Leah said, Is it nothing that you've taken my husband? Rachel said, If you do, you can have him tonight. So that night Jacob lay with Leah. God heard her and she had a son, Issachar, then another, Zebulun, and afterward a daughter, Dinah. Then God remembered Rachel and unlocked her womb. She had a son and called him Joseph.

Jacob heads home

After Joseph's birth, Jacob told Laban, Release me. Give me my wives and children, I'll go home. He took Rachel and Leah to the fields and said, I see your father eyeing me differently. You know I served him well though he toyed with me, changed my wages often—yet my father's God never let him hurt me. God even took his cattle and gave them to me. They replied, We've no part in our father's house. He treated us as foreigners, sold us, and kept the entire price. Anything God strips from him is ours. So Jacob put his sons and wives on camels and drove his herds and property toward Canaan. Meanwhile, Rachel had stolen her family's idols. When Laban heard, he chased and overtook them. He said, What've you done, lying and herding my daughters like war booty. I'd have thrown you a feast and kissed them good-bye. But so be it. Yet, why steal my family idols? Jacob said, I feared you'd snatch your daughters back. But whoever took the idols will die. (He didn't know Rachel had them.) Laban searched Jacob's tent, Leah's, the handmaids', then went to Rachel's. They were in a camel cushion she was sitting on. She said, Forgive me, I can't rise, I have my period. So he found nothing. He told Jacob, What can I do? Let's make a pact. Next morning he kissed his family, blessed them, and went home.

Jacob and the man

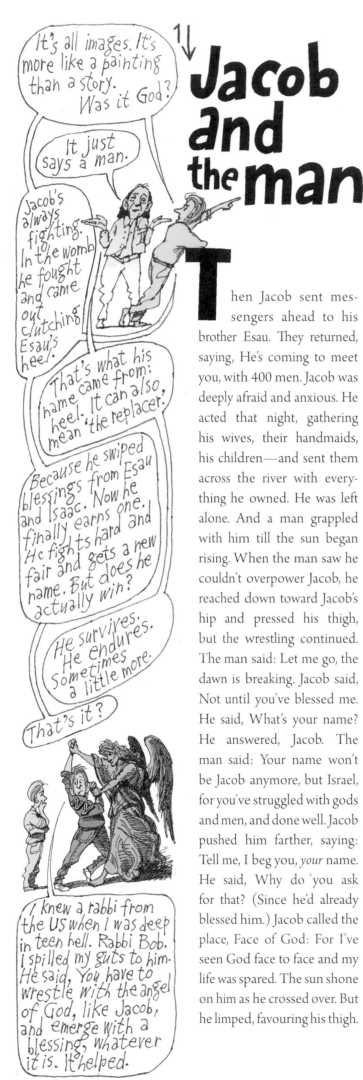

Then Jacob sent messengers ahead to his brother Esau. They returned, saying, He's coming to meet you, with 400 men. Jacob was deeply afraid and anxious. He acted that night, gathering his wives, their handmaids, his children—and sent them across the river with everything he owned. He was left alone. And a man grappled with him till the sun began rising. When the man saw he couldn't overpower Jacob, he reached down toward Jacob's hip and pressed his thigh, but the wrestling continued. The man said: Let me go, the dawn is breaking. Jacob said, Not until you've blessed me. He said, What's your name? He answered, Jacob. The man said: Your name won't be Jacob anymore, but Israel, for you've struggled with gods and men, and done well. Jacob pushed him farther, saying: Tell me, I beg you, *your* name. He said, Why do you ask for that? (Since he'd already blessed him.) Jacob called the place, Face of God: For I've seen God face to face and my life was spared. The sun shone on him as he crossed over. But he limped, favouring his thigh.

The brothers meet again

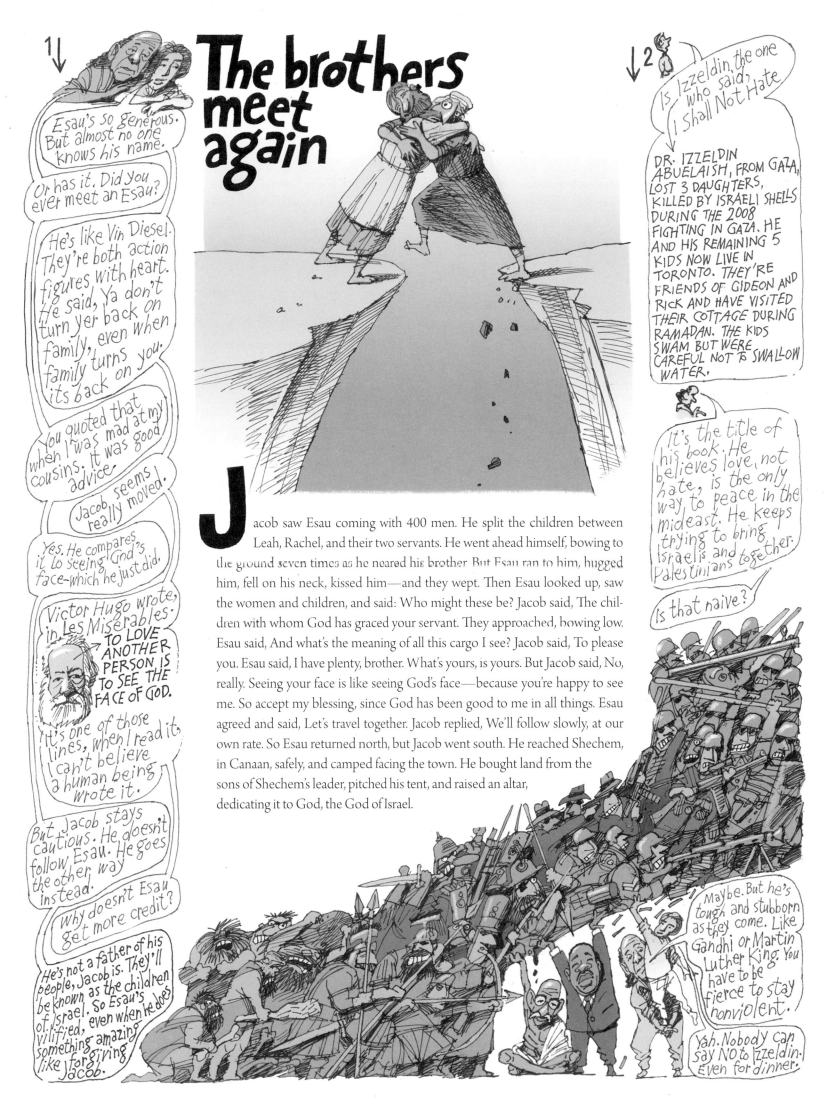

1↓

Esau's so generous. But almost no one knows his name.

Or has it. Did you ever meet an Esau?

He's like Vin Diesel. They're both action figures with heart. He said, Ya don't turn yer back on family, even when family turns its back on you.

You quoted that when I was mad at my cousins. It was good advice.

Jacob seems really moved.

Yes. He compares it to seeing God's face—which he just did.

Victor Hugo wrote, in Les Misérables, TO LOVE ANOTHER PERSON IS TO SEE THE FACE OF GOD.

It's one of those lines, when I read it, I can't believe a human being wrote it.

But Jacob stays cautious. He doesn't follow Esau. He goes the other way instead.

Why doesn't Esau get more credit?

He's not a father of his people, Jacob is. They'll be known as the children of Israel. So Esau's vilified, even when he does something amazing like forgiving Jacob.

↓2

Is Izzeldin, the one who said, I Shall Not Hate

DR. IZZELDIN ABUELAISH, FROM GAZA, LOST 3 DAUGHTERS, KILLED BY ISRAELI SHELLS DURING THE 2008 FIGHTING IN GAZA. HE AND HIS REMAINING 5 KIDS NOW LIVE IN TORONTO. THEY'RE FRIENDS OF GIDEON AND RICK AND HAVE VISITED THEIR COTTAGE DURING RAMADAN. THE KIDS SWAM BUT WERE CAREFUL NOT TO SWALLOW WATER.

It's the title of his book. He believes love, not hate, is the only way to peace in the mideast. He keeps trying to bring Israelis and Palestinians together.

Is that naive?

Maybe. But he's tough and stubborn as they come. Like Gandhi or Martin Luther King. You have to be fierce to stay nonviolent.

Yah. Nobody can say NO to Izzeldin. Even for dinner.

Jacob saw Esau coming with 400 men. He split the children between Leah, Rachel, and their two servants. He went ahead himself, bowing to the ground seven times as he neared his brother. But Esau ran to him, hugged him, fell on his neck, kissed him—and they wept. Then Esau looked up, saw the women and children, and said: Who might these be? Jacob said, The children with whom God has graced your servant. They approached, bowing low. Esau said, And what's the meaning of all this cargo I see? Jacob said, To please you. Esau said, I have plenty, brother. What's yours, is yours. But Jacob said, No, really. Seeing your face is like seeing God's face—because you're happy to see me. So accept my blessing, since God has been good to me in all things. Esau agreed and said, Let's travel together. Jacob replied, We'll follow slowly, at our own rate. So Esau returned north, but Jacob went south. He reached Shechem, in Canaan, safely, and camped facing the town. He bought land from the sons of Shechem's leader, pitched his tent, and raised an altar, dedicating it to God, the God of Israel.

The land of Israel

When he was a student, Rick spent a year in the Land of Israel, or Palestine, as others know it. He loved it. He learned Hebrew and studied everything: Bible, Talmud, Jewish mysticism (Kabbalah), medieval Hebrew love poetry, modern Hebrew literature. He was a sponge, a glutton. He visited socialist kibbutzim and ultra-Orthodox villages. When he went home, he thought he'd go back and live there.

Then he never returned, decade after decade.

When Gideon was thirteen, they travelled to the Land of Israel together. At the airport, the border official asked, like border officials everywhere:

Rick felt they'd always known each other, though they'd never met.

After he and Gideon had visited the Western Wall,

← THE ONLY SURVIVING PART OF THE TEMPLE THAT THE ROMANS DESTROYED IN 70 A.D.

and the Dead Sea,

A BUOYANT SALT WATER LAKE IN THE DESERT.

GIDEON FLOATED IN IT.

and Masada, →

THE DESERT FORTRESS WHERE JEWISH MARTYRS FOUGHT THEIR LAST BATTLE IN THE REBELLION AGAINST ROME

Rick said he thought he finally understood why he'd stayed away so long.

I used to think it was because I disagreed with Israeli policies like the occupation. But I disagree with US policies and I go there lots.

Then why?

Embarrassment, I think. When I lived here I was enthralled. I camped on Biblical sites. I spent everything I had on Hebrew books. I danced through Jerusalem with Orthodox Jews on Simchat Torah.

THE 'BIRTHDAY' OF THE TORAH WHEN THE TWIN SCROLLS GET ROLLED BACK FROM MOSES' DEATH, AT THE END, ALL THE WAY TO 'WHEN GOD BEGAN CREATING...'

Then I left it behind and I feel weird about changing so much so fast. Who was that guy? Was he needy? Who's this one? Is he shallow? But you helped me overcome that.

You help me see what really matters, like sharing whoever I am, with people I love. So what if I'm embarrassed or confused?

HOW?

That's life, as they say.

L'chayim, as they say.

The rape of Dinah

Holy crap.

Yeah.

How did they teach you this when you were a kid?

They didn't.

She never speaks. She has no say. Her family acts 'for' her.

It's primitive payback, families used to avenge their own. Eventually Moses comes along and gives laws to make it more just.

But when the legal system fails, do you act anyway?

That's still the issue.

Besides, acting for Dinah without her consent just magnifies her silence. And that kind of silence can lead to more rape.

Leah's daughter, Dinah, went out to view the local women. Shechem, the prince of the place, saw her. He grabbed her, forced her down, and humiliated her. Yet he was drawn to her. He loved her and spoke intimately to her. He told his father, Hamor, Get me this girl as a wife. Jacob learned of the rape. His sons were away so he stalled till they returned. When they heard, they were furious. It was obscene, unthinkable. But Hamor said, My son's heart yearns for her. Please, give her to him as a wife. Give us your daughters and take ours. Live here, the land will lie before you. Trade in it, own it. Shechem himself said, May it please you, ask and I'll do anything. Jacob's sons replied craftily, for he'd raped their sister: Giving her to an uncircumcised man would be shameful. But we'll agree—if you become like us, circumcising all males. Then we'll join you as one people. That sounded good to Hamor and his son, who wasted no time, since he ached for Dinah. So each male was circumcised. Three days later, while they were still in pain, Jacob's sons, Simon and Levi, took swords, entered unimpeded, and slaughtered every male. They took Dinah and left. They stripped the corpses and plundered the town: flocks, herds, donkeys. Their wealth, little ones, wives. Jacob said, You've made me stink among the people of this land. My numbers are few, they'll unite and destroy me—and my house. But they answered, Can he treat our sister as a whore?

But they do support her. They don't say she 'provoked' it.

Yah. They support her in that sense.

And it doesn't condone rape, at least not their sister's.

What's wrong is that the sexism behind her rape gets reinforced by her silence. Things won't ever change if that remains. It's like the guy at the airport in Israel said.

Same problems?

Same problems.

Rachel and Isaac at the end

They travelled on. While they were still on the way, Rachel gave birth. It was a difficult labour. When it was at its hardest, the midwife said, Don't worry, you have another son. As her soul was leaving (for she was dying), she called him Ben-Oni, Son of My Suffering, but Jacob called him Benjamin. She died, and was buried. Jacob placed a monument over her grave. It's still there. While they were in that place, Reuben went and slept with Bilhah, his father's concubine, and Jacob heard about it. By then he had twelve sons. He went to see his father Isaac in Hebron, where both he and Abraham had dwelled. Isaac had lived 180 years. He breathed his last, died, and was gathered to his people, old and filled with experiences. Esau and Jacob, his sons, buried him.

I like the women. Sarah's funny, Rebekah's tough, Rachel's a handful. I wish they said more before they die.

It's as if they dropped in briefly from another Bible.

The women's Bible.

You could make a Bible with all the stuff left out of the Bible.

Like Reuben and Bilhah, Jacob's concubine—what's with that?

Exactly. Just one line.

He's firstborn, right? Maybe he's staking his claim. The firstborns don't have great prospects. And we never hear Bilhah's voice. Just like Dinah.

That'd be in the other Bible. From here on, it's mostly about Jacob's sons. Jacob, sort of, he never fades, but he never goes away.

That's Jacob. Flickers but doesn't fail.

He survives, and gives his people their name. The people of Israel.

↓1

I like 'gathered to his people.' But what does it mean?

He went where everyone goes when they die. Nowhere, back into the pool, or, in this case, of everybody, his people.

It sounds like recycled.

It's my own interpretation, I grant.

What about going to heaven?

In the Bible heaven is the sky. There's no real afterlife. You live on in your people, the ones your life was part of, whether it's your family or your group. In their memories of you. Especially if you were the first in the line.

That **is** an afterlife. You're not there to see it, but you're there.

Maybe it's because he actually made them up, to get back at his brothers for hating him. It isn't Joseph's fault that his father loves him more.

My teacher Nehama said the stories become more secular now. She meant the characters make their own choices. God doesn't always intervene.

Jacob lived where his father had, in Canaan. Joseph, who was seventeen, tended his father's flocks, helping the sons of Zilpah and Bilhah, his father's wives, and he brought nasty rumours about them to their father. Israel loved Joseph over all his sons because he was the child of his old age, so he made him a fancy jacket. His brothers saw their father loved him most, and hated him. They couldn't even stand speaking to him nicely. Then Joseph dreamed a dream, told them, and they hated him even more. He said, Listen to this dream: we're binding sheaves in the field and mine rose up tall, while all yours bowed down around it. His brothers said, So you'll rule us and lord it over us? Then he had another dream that he told them: In it, the sun and moon and eleven stars are bowing down to me. He told his father too, who scolded him, saying, What's this dream? Will I and your mother and brothers all bow to the ground before you? So his brothers were jealous while his father did nothing, for the moment.

You mean interfere. The way he did in the garden or the flood or with Abraham, telling him to get out of his homeland and sacrifice his son.

Nehama was a pious person. She thought God stayed involved but more through what she called 'divine providence' instead of jumping in directly.

Sounds like progress. Even parents sometimes learn that.

Joseph and the man

The man's spooky. He's like 'the man' Jacob wrestles. How does he know who Joseph's brothers are? Why's he even there?

The rabbinic commentaries say it shows God is guiding things indirectly. He's an angel or messenger.

Then why didn't God have him tell the brothers to stay put?

Hm. THOMAS MANN wrote 4 novels called 'Joseph and his Brothers.' He turned this meeting into an all-night conversation between Joseph and 'the man' about the meaning of life as they walk in the dark.

Did you ever wander at night when you lived there? Was it spooky?

My first night in Jerusalem I was walking across some empty hills to meet friends at a restaurant. I had to pee and I thought, I can't do that.

Why not?

It was the holy land. I was very religious.

What did you do?

I peed. I thought: what would Abraham or King David have done?

Life goes on.

His brothers went to shepherd their father's flock in Shechem. Israel said to Joseph, You know your brothers are herding in Shechem. Get moving, I'm sending you to them. I'm ready, Joseph answered. See how they and the flock are doing, said Jacob, and bring me word. So he sent Joseph off from the Hebron Valley and he reached Shechem. A man found him wandering in the field there and asked, What are you looking for? He said, I'm looking for my brothers, can you tell me where they're pasturing? The man said, They moved on from here—I heard them say, Let's go to Dotan. So Joseph went after them, and caught up with them in Dotan.

Yeah. Even when God's speaking or the ground's holy.

I like how little is said here. It's like when God asks Cain, 'Where's your brother?' Cain says, 'How do I know?'

There are strange moments in the Bible that just happen. It's like a loud noise in a cave but there's no noise. It's sometimes called echo. It's 'numinous.' Something strange breaks into the plane we live on. It seems to come from somewhere else, then it goes away. You can't do much except gawk.

WITTGENSTEIN said: THAT WHEREOF WE CANNOT SPEAK, WE MUST THEREOF BE SILENT. He was on my course.

A great philosopher of language.

Because he knew when to shut up.

Jacob in mourning, Joseph in Egypt

↓1

Why don't they give Joseph credit instead of saying over and over that God did it for him? Maybe he was a good manager.

There's a religious tradition that wealth flows from God as a reward to his believers. In Christianity it's called the Prosperity Gospel. You see it in those ostentatious megachurches on TV.

That's illogical. Jesus said he came to help the poor, not the rich.

If religions had to be consistent, they'd never have lasted this long.

You mean, like how Jacob says Joseph's in the underworld even though you told me there's no afterlife in the Bible.

Excellent example.

Religions are so variable—how do you even know what they are?

You don't. They're all over the map...

You studied religion, in grad school and the seminary.

Seminaries, plural. Jewish and Protestant. I couldn't get enough.

↓2

Then define religion.

Definitions are overrated. They always come after the thing exists and never quite fit.

What was the point of studying it? You can't even say what it is.

But, as the judge said about pornography, I know it when I see it.

God's become kind of indirect and impersonal. In the old days, he'd have dropped by and had a chat with Joseph, like he did with Abraham.

He's still a force here but he acts from a distance.

That makes God sound like gravity. Or fate. He used to be a pain but I sort of miss his meddling. It was so human.

He'll be back. The Bible fluctuates. Sometimes God's in your face. Face to face, as it often says. Then he's not. The Joseph stories are about people—they are more like a novel, though they keep shoehorning God in.

Shoehorning?

Never mind.

They took the fancy jacket and sent it to their father saying, We found this, do you recognize it? He did, crying, My son's jacket! A hideous beast has eaten him, torn him apart. O Joseph! Then Jacob ripped his clothes, wrapped himself in mourning rags, and mourned his son for many days. All his sons and daughters came to comfort him but he refused, saying, No, it would be better for me to go down and join him in the underworld. So he mourned and he wept.

Meanwhile Joseph was taken down to Egypt, where Potiphar, a high official of Pharaoh, bought him. God was with Joseph, who found success in his Egyptian master's house. His master saw that God was with him, causing him to prosper. So he gave Joseph control over his household and all he had. From the moment he appointed Joseph, God blessed his house, for Joseph's sake. God's blessing was on it all, both the home and the fields. So his master left everything in Joseph's hands, paying no attention, beyond the meals he was served.

The seduction of Joseph

1↓

Joseph was the first Hebrew slave in Egypt but not the last. Generations later, Moses led his whole nation of slaves out of Egypt.

On Passover! Seders recreate it.

But Joseph was a privileged slave, he had power.

A slave's a slave. Being a few steps higher on the ladder doesn't change that.

It even brings special problems. A Canadian worker-poet wrote about writers who get wellpaid to serve the powerful:

'A MAN IN CHAINS MAY YET BE BRAVE THE MEANEST IS THE MENTAL SLAVE.'

Joseph had fine features and looked good. His master's wife stared at him and said, Lie with me. Joseph refused, saying, My master trusts me with his household. He's put all he has in my control. No one is greater here. He's withheld nothing but you, his wife. How could I do this great evil—and sin against God? She pestered Joseph daily but he wouldn't lie with her. Then one day, he came to work in the house with none of the staff present. She grabbed at his clothing and said, Lie with me. He left it in her hand and fled outside. When she saw he'd left his clothes, she called the staff, saying, Look, your master brought a Hebrew here who is mocking us. He came to lie with me but I screamed. When he heard that, he left his clothes and ran. Then she put them aside till her husband returned. She said, Your Hebrew slave came to have sex with me. But when I screamed, he ran out, leaving his clothes. When he heard that, he was furious. He handed Joseph over to the special prison where the king's prisoners were held. So there he was, in jail.

↓2

I remember when I learned you'd been in jail. I asked why you and Clayton were friends. You said he was an old friend who got you out of jail.

You were 5 or 6. I could see it bothered you.

I knew it was during a strike, helping workers fight for justice. And I knew Robin Hood, the outlaw, was a good guy. Still, it unsettled me.

A while later we were listening to PETER, PAUL AND MARY in the car:

Nothing substitutes for freedom.

"Have you been to jail for justice? I want to shake your hand."

You leaned forward in your carseat:

You've been to jail for justice!

Yes.

I want to shake your hand!

Maybe the song, or just that it was on a CD, made me feel OK.

You rose to the challenge.

There's a box of papers in our basement labelled Dreams in a Box! Are they yours?

Uh, yes.

Did you predict the future from them, like Joseph?

God no. I was just trying to figure out what was going on in my head.

Did it work?

I have no idea. I never reread them. It was a thing you did in therapy.

You wanted to know what you were thinking when you weren't actually thinking.

That sounds right.

Joseph in jail

God was with Joseph, who found favour in the warden's eyes. He put the other prisoners under Joseph's control. Then the king's cupbearer and baker offended Pharaoh. He fumed and put them in the prison. One night they both dreamed. That morning Joseph saw they were troubled. He asked, Why the grim faces? We dreamed, they said, but the meaning's unclear. He said, Meanings belong to God. Tell me. The cupbearer recounted, There's a vine, on it are 3 branches. It flowers, blooms, and its clusters ripen. Pharaoh's cup is in my hand. I squeeze grapes into it and hand it to Pharaoh. Joseph said, The branches are 3 days. Then Pharaoh will restore you. But remember me, please, when things go well. Mention me to Pharaoh and get me out. For I was cruelly stolen from the land of the Hebrews, and here too, I did no wrong. Yet they threw me in this pit.

Joseph's more practical. He's gone from one pit to another. His dreams got him into the first. Now he hopes other people's dreams get him out.

The poor baker hears the cupbearer get good news so he decides to try his luck. But Joseph tells him he's going to be beheaded.

I like that about Joseph. He doesn't try to smooth it over. He used to be a dick when he talked about dreams, but he's getting more like his father. Smart and wily.

Basically, you shouldn't judge people just on what they are but on all the stuff they had to overcome to get there.

Like Pete Seeger said.

WE SHALL OVERCOME.

The baker saw Joseph interpreted the dream hopefully and said, In mine, 3 baskets are on my head. The top one has pastries for Pharaoh. Birds are eating them. Joseph said, The baskets are 3 days. Then Pharaoh will lop off your head and hang you from a tree, while birds eat your flesh. 3 days later, on Pharaoh's birthday, he gave a banquet. He restored the cupbearer and hanged the baker, as Joseph said. But the cupbearer didn't remember Joseph. He forgot him.

Joseph makes his move

Two years later, Pharaoh dreamed. He's by the Nile. Seven cattle, fine and fleshy, feed in the reeds. 7 others, sickly and scrawny, come and eat them. He awoke, then dreamed again: 7 ears of corn on one stalk, healthy and good. Then 7 thin ears, rotted by an east wind. The 7 thin ears swallow the good. In the morning, his heart pounded. He called Egypt's diviners, but none could explain them. Then his cupbearer spoke: Today I recall my sins. Pharaoh raged at his servants and imprisoned me and the baker. One night we both dreamed. With us was a young Hebrew. We told him. He explained our dreams, and what he said came true. Pharaoh sent for Joseph. They hurried him out of that pit. He shaved, changed clothes, and came. Pharaoh said, I dreamed but the meaning's unclear. I hear you explain dreams. Joseph said: Not I but God will calm Pharaoh down. He has revealed what he'll do. The 7 good cows and good ears are 7 years. So are the scrawny cattle and withered ears. 7 years of plenty approach. 7 years of famine will follow. The plenty will be forgotten as famine destroys the land. So let Pharaoh find a wise man and set him over Egypt. Let him appoint officials. Have them gather food in the good years, store it in the cities, and guard it—so there will be food during famine. That sounded good to Pharaoh. He said, Will we find another like this, with God's spirit? So Pharaoh said, You shall stand over my house, through your word my people will be governed. Only I will be greater. Pharaoh took his ring and put it on Joseph's finger. He wrapped him in fine clothes and laid a gold chain round his neck. He had him

44

ride in a chariot while they cried out before him. Pharaoh gave Joseph the name Tzafnat-Paneah, and Asnat, daughter of the priest of On, as his wife. Joseph was thirty. He travelled throughout Egypt. The land produced much in the good years, which Joseph gathered, brought to the cities, and stored—like the sand of the sea. He had two sons: Manasseh and Ephraim. The 7 good years ended and famine began. It spread everywhere, but in Egypt there was grain. So when Egypt hungered and people cried for bread, Pharaoh said, Go to Joseph. He opened the storehouses and sold to them. The whole world came to Egypt, and to Joseph, to buy food.

I like how we suddenly find out there's been an interpreter between them. We don't know that till the end. It's like the camera pulls back and you realize there's this complex emotional situation— all passing through translation!

Joseph looks and speaks Egyptian. Of course they didn't recognize him.

Plus they think he's dead. He's the last guy they expect to find running Egypt. They have no idea he understands every word they say.

Being translated is a weird experience. Your mind wanders a bit while you wait. Time sort of slows down.

2

So it gives Joseph room to remember his dream about them bowing to him – and now they really are.

But not the way he expected it to happen.

Of course not. He was just a kid then.

And it gives the brothers room to go into a panic. They remember Joseph begging for his life, from the pit, and they wouldn't listen.

I don't think we knew that detail before. They just let him scream. It shows how much they must've hated him!

Or didn't care.

Or enjoyed it—

They repressed that moment but now it gushes out too, along with their guilt, as if it was waiting all this time to jump them.

You have a good nose for guilt. I sometimes think you like it.

I wouldn't say I like it. But I get it.

He knows, they don't

Jacob said to his sons, Why do you sit around stupidly? I hear there's corn in Egypt, go buy some so we'll survive. Ten of Joseph's brothers went. Jacob kept Benjamin, in case something awful happened. So the sons of Israel were among those who came to Egypt. Joseph was in charge. His brothers arrived and bowed to the ground before him. He recognized them but they didn't recognize him. And Joseph recalled his dreams. He snapped, You're spies. They said, No, master. We're honest sons of one man; only the smallest remains with his father, and another is no longer. Joseph said, This will be your test: one of you will be imprisoned while the rest take food home. Then bring your youngest brother back to confirm your claims. Each cried to his brother, This is punishment for what we did to our brother, whose distress we saw when he begged for mercy and we didn't respond. Reuben said, I told you not to sin against the child, but you wouldn't listen. They didn't know Joseph understood their words, since there was an interpreter between them. He turned away and wept, then turned back, ordering that Simon be held. He was bound as they watched.

J

oseph ordered their bags filled with grain, and their money put back in each pack. They loaded the grain and left. When they opened their packs along the way, each saw his silver—and their hearts faltered. They trembled, saying, What is God doing? When they reached Jacob in Canaan, they described what happened. They were terrified. Jacob said, You're killing me. Joseph is no more, and Simon, now you'll take Benjamin. Reuben said, Kill my two sons if I don't return him. Jacob said, He's not going. But famine continued weighing on the land. When they'd finished the grain, their father said, Go again, buy a bit more. Judah replied, If you're willing to send our brother, we'll go. If not, we won't. For that man said, You won't see my face without your brother. Israel said, Why did you tell him you have another brother? Judah answered, Send him, I guarantee his safety. It'll be on me—forever. Their father said, Well, if you're going, take some of the best of the land: honey, raisins, pistachios, almonds. And twice the silver, with what came back in your packs. Maybe it was a mistake. And yes, all right, your brother. Get going. As for me: if I must mourn again, I will.

Jacob gives in

47

It's like a dense Russian novel. Emotions, thoughts, details. What happened to that sparse, unemotional style, like the sacrifice of Isaac?

Scholars say different Biblical styles come from different sources.

Meaning what?

They say the Bible combines versions from different times and places, sometimes several in a single verse. They code them by letters like P for a source written by priests. Seminary students I knew used to mark up their Bibles with hi-liters— well, not hi-liters, coloured pencils— till they looked like rainbows.

It sounds ridiculous. People change their hair styles and clothes all the time but they're still one person.

True. Theatre director PETER BROOK said the classics in art often have no style. They go with whatever works. Shakespeare mixes tragic and comic all the time. He's too busy telling stories with gusto to bother defining his 'style'.

You could hi-lite Hamlet—if you had nothing better to do.

So they took it all, and Benjamin. They returned and stood before Joseph. He saw Benjamin and told his household chief, Take them home, they'll dine with me at noon. He did. They were terrified. They said, They've brought us here to seize and enslave us—even our donkeys. They told the household chief, Please sir, we came only for grain. We've no idea how the silver got there. He said, Rest easy. It was a gift from your god. Your silver stayed here. Then he brought Simon out, took them inside, gave them water, washed their feet, and fed their donkeys. They prepared their tribute. Joseph arrived and they offered it, bowing low. He asked how they were and, How is your aged father? Does he still live? They said, He is alive and well. They prostrated themselves again. He looked up and saw Benjamin, son of his own mother. He said, May God favour you, my boy. Then he rushed away. He was overwhelmed, so he stepped into another room and wept. He washed his face, went back out, fought for composure, and said, Serve the meal. He ate separately, with the Egyptians, since Egyptians couldn't eat with Israelites. It was considered sacrilegious. He had them seated in order of age. That amazed them. Servings arrived, with Benjamin's five times larger. Everyone drank till they were drunk.

I like how Joseph still loves his family.

Why? They were cruel to him, and he hasn't seen them in years!

Yeah but that doesn't matter.

RICK HAD A BAD RELATIONSHIP WITH HIS DAD, WHICH HURT HIS RELATIONSHIP WITH THE REST OF HIS FAMILY. HE DOESN'T GET ALONG WITH MOST OF THEM TODAY.

GIDEON HAS A BIG FAMILY ON HIS MOM'S SIDE. HE'S PARTICULARLY CLOSE TO HIS COUSINS JAKE AND CHARLOTTE, EVEN THOUGH THEY ONLY SEE EACH OTHER ONCE OR TWICE A YEAR.

'Ya don't turn yer back on family even when family...'

Bloody Vin Diesel. Did he have to be so right?

The goblet in Benjamin's pack

↓1

It's like Joseph's playing God with them. He creates the same situation as when they threw Joseph in the pit. Except this time with Benjamin, Rachel's other son, who Jacob loves just as much. Then he waits, to see what they do.

That's what God gets, for creating beings 'in his image.' They **create** too.

But why does Joseph make them repeat the pattern?

The traditional answer is, he's giving them a chance to repent for what they did to him long ago.

That's so goody-goody religious. I see Joseph as a more practical guy.

It could be revenge. He's making them suffer the way they did to him.

↓2

Or he doesn't know why but he does it. People repeat things all the time that made them miserable even if it just makes them more miserable.

Repetition compulsion.

It has a name? Who said that—Freud?

I never believed it. I think we recreate the past because we want to get it right next time. Joseph may hope his brothers act better, with another chance.

And himself. He made some blunders I bet he'd like to have back.

I think that's why I returned to Toronto after being away so long. Things happened when I was growing up that I wanted to revisit so I could fix them.

That was over 40 years ago. How did it go? Did you figure it all out?

I might be starting to.

Then he ordered his chief to fill each sack with food, place silver at the top—And put my silver goblet with the youngest. At dawn they left. They hadn't gone far when Joseph told his man, Pursue them and say: Why did you repay good with evil? Hasn't my master's goblet—the one he foretells the future with—been snatched? He overtook them and said so. They replied, Why would he say that? Heaven forbid we did it. The silver we found, we returned. Why would we take anything more from his house? Whoever's found with it, let him die. The rest will become slaves. He said, So be it. Then he searched each pack, starting with the eldest and ending with Benjamin. And the goblet was in his. They tore their clothes, loaded their donkeys, returned to Joseph's house—he was still there—and fell on the ground before him. He said, What've you done? Didn't you know I'd discover it? Judah said, What can we say, what words could justify us? God has exposed our guilt. Consider us your slaves, along with he who had the goblet. But Joseph said, I wouldn't think of that. The one with the goblet becomes my slave. The rest, go in peace to your father.

Why the shift?

When Jacob said, 'My wife only gave me two sons'—he insulted his other wives and his other sons. But Judah doesn't sound bitter about it like he used to. He seems to accept it.

Maybe because the stakes are so high. He has to stay calm.

Or he's wiser. He doesn't argue about how the goblet got into the pack either. He focusses on other things, especially the family.

It sounds like he's speaking as much about what happened to Joseph as about Benjamin. He implies the brothers will be guilty about both—'forever.'

Judah's monologue

Judah approached, saying,

Please hear me, lord, and don't be angry, for you are like Pharaoh. My lord asked: Have you still a father, or brother? We answered: An aged father, and a child of his old age, who alone remains from his mother, and our father adores him. You said, Bring him here, so I can see him. We said: He can't leave his father, who would die without him. But you said: If he doesn't come, you won't see me again. When we told Jacob our father, he said: You know my wife gave me two sons. One went away and I believe was torn apart, for I've never seen him since. If you take this one and some disaster occurs, you'll have driven my wretched grey head down into the dust. Now if I return—and the youth not with us, and his life so enmeshed with his father's—it'll be like lowering our father into his grave. I guaranteed the lad's safety, saying: If I don't return him to you, father, I'll have sinned against you forever. So let me replace him as my lord's slave, while he returns with his brothers. For how can I go back without the boy, to see my father destroyed by it?

Buber said in the Hassidic tradition—

HASSIDISM BEGAN AS A MOVEMENT THAT VALUED THE FEELINGS OF POOR AND ORDINARY JEWS, EVEN THOUGH THEY WEREN'T LEARNED RABBIS.

The source of all conflict between me and my fellow humans is that I don't say what I mean and I don't do what I say.

MARTIN BUBER

He meant you can cut through a quarrel by saying what you really feel.

Like what?

Like: I don't believe you really love me. Or: I'm still angry for something you did long ago.

Hm. Do you think that would've helped your relationship with mum? You can change things by saying what's in your heart. But not always.

And by itself alone it won't end a conflict. Because conflicts have two sides. This one depends on Joseph now, he has to speak from his heart too.

The move to Egypt

A report of this went to Pharaoh. It seemed good in his eyes. He told Joseph, Gather your father and your households and bring them. I'll give them the best land in Egypt. Joseph provided wagons and food for the journey. So his brothers returned to Canaan, and Jacob. They said, Joseph still lives—he rules Egypt! Jacob's heart pounded and he didn't believe it. But they told him everything, he saw the wagons Joseph sent—and his spirit was revived. He said, How great it is that Joseph lives, I'll go and see him before I die. So the children of Israel brought Jacob, their little ones, wives, herds, and everything they had. Joseph harnessed his chariot and went to meet Israel his father in the province of Goshen. He fell on Jacob's neck and wept on it once more. Israel said, Now I can die, having seen your face, for you still live. Joseph said, I will tell Pharaoh: My brothers and father's household have come. They are shepherds and herders, as they've always been, they've brought their flocks and herds. When Pharaoh asks: What do you do? Answer him: We've been herders from our youth until now, us and our fathers—so that he'll have you remain far away out here in Goshen. Because the Egyptians detest shepherds.

They hate shepherds?

Egypt was a rich, ancient empire. It had officials, armies, pyramids. It relied on farmers in the fertile Nile delta for food and forced labour. They were easy to control because they were stuck on their land. Shepherds were more independent types. If they didn't like being ruled, they could just move on.

Poor Jacob. Regaining his hope that Joseph's alive almost kills him.

Hope can be harder to live with than hopelessness.

Because you can crash again. It takes guts to keep hoping.

So true. I ended a play with: "Cheer up, there's no hope." It was about a messiah who turned out to be false. Those were his final words to his followers. He hoped it would make them feel better. And it did.

So he ended up not being so false.

HERDERS

Farming let them develop and diversify their civilizations but it also led to tyranny. Shepherds were freer, but their way of life was less complex.

So powerful governments preferred farmers over shepherds.

Cain, the first farmer murdered his brother, Abel, the shepherd. Does the Bible mean their ways of life were bound to clash?

It's just an interpretation. But the first Israelite king, David, began as a shepherd boy who became a hero to his people. Then, as their king, he started messing up. As if the shepherd in him fought with the king he became.

That sounds like a good story.

One of the best.

52

Jacob's blessing

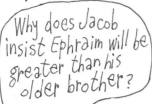

1 ↓

Why does Jacob insist Ephraim will be greater than his older brother?

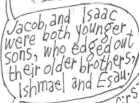

↓ 2

Jacob, and Isaac were both younger sons, who edged out their older brothers, Ishmael and Esau.

Even with the first two brothers, Abel was younger but God favoured his offering so Cain killed him out of jealousy.

The Bible can't stand primogeniture— the idea that the firstborn inherits the father's wealth and position. It's an upstart religion with an upstart god and it fought to overthrow traditional ways. Jacob even raises Joseph's sons to the level of his brothers. The Bible favours the younger sibling— male sibling of course— every chance it gets.

But Ephraim isn't especially deserving. It's not like Manasseh did something wrong. Jacob's just replacing one random system with another.

What would Tom think about all this?

TOM IS A FRIEND OF GIDEON'S FROM ENGLAND. HIS FAMILY IS IN THE ARISTOCRACY THERE AND HE'S TECHNICALLY A LORD. HIS OLDER BROTHER, AN EARL, RANKS ABOVE HIM.

This is a different time, Tom's almost embarrassed by it all. It's not like him and his brother were any different when they were babies.

OK, but at least the Bible challenges how things were. Pharaohs, kings, patriarchs— inherited their positions. It's good to undermine old rules.

Israel settled in Egypt, in Goshen region. They were fruitful and multiplied there. Israel's death drew near. He summoned Joseph saying, Don't bury me here, I want to lie with my fathers. Some time later, Joseph was told, Your father is sick. So he came with his two boys. Israel gathered his strength and sat up in bed. He said, Your two sons, born before I came here, shall be my very own. Have them approach and I'll bless them. But his eyes were heavy with age, he couldn't see. So he pulled them near, kissing and hugging them. He said, I never expected to see you again—now God's even shown me your children. Joseph drew them back, positioning Ephraim, with his right hand, to Jacob's left, and Manasseh, with his left hand, to Jacob's right, then moved them forward. But Israel reached out his right hand, placing it on Ephraim's head, though he was younger, and his left on Manasseh's—crossing his hands, though Manasseh was the firstborn—and blessed them. Joseph saw it. It seemed wrong. So he took his father's hand to move it over, saying, Not so, father, this one is the firstborn. But his father resisted, saying, I know, my son, I know. He'll have a great future too. But his younger brother will be greater still.

Well, if you want to put it that way.

That's just making trouble for its own sake. But you are kind of an anarchist. I think what counts is fair treatment whether you're older or not.

An end

Jacob called his other sons, saying, I'll tell you what will happen to you in the end of days. He blessed each with his own blessing and ordered, Bury me with my fathers. Then he curled up on his bed, breathed his last, and was gathered to his people. Joseph sent word to Pharaoh saying, My father had me swear to bury him in Canaan. So they went, grieved with great and grave wailing, and returned. Joseph's brothers worried, with their father dead, Will he now despise us, and pay us back for what we did to him? So they announced, Your father told us before he died to say: Please forgive your brothers' sin. Joseph wept at that. His brothers fell before him and said, We'll be your slaves. Joseph replied, Do I stand in God's place? You wished evil on me but God wished good—to bring us to this day and give birth to a great people. So don't be afraid, I'll support you and your little ones. They remained in Egypt and Joseph lived till 120. Then he said, I am dying. He had the children of Israel swear, saying, You shall bring my bones from this place—and he died. He was embalmed and put in a coffin.

That's not all

Gideon the skeptic

Gideon the democrat

ACKNOWLEDGEMENTS

Many thanks to Jack David, who supported this rather unusual and challenging project from the start, through many trials, and never wavered in his commitment and good humour. He joined others in creating ECW, an institution that retains the earliest, best impulses of independent publishing. Thanks to everyone there as well.

Deep gratitude to Sarah Polley, who's been a great friend of the project from the start, and to Janette Luu, who joined at a crucial moment to assure it remained on track.

Thanks to the many friends and supporters who saw the potential in the idea, including Rabbi Yael Splansky, Liz Wolfe and Yoni Goldstein. And to all the donors who contributed to the campaign that made its completion possible.

Special thanks to Rosa Sarabia, the best reader a writer could have, whose insights and fine visual sense were invaluable.

To Margaret Atwood, for her beautiful foreword, only matched in its depth and generosity by her lifelong friendship to us both.

And to Dušan Petričić, who stands in the great tradition, like Daumier, of illustrator and commentator. He has become, to both of us, a soulmate and brother.

Rick Salutin
Gideon Salutin

Rosa Sarabia

RICK SALUTIN is a playwright, novelist, and journalist who has received awards in all these areas. He wrote a weekly column for *The Globe and Mail* for 20 years and now provides weekly columns and videos for the *Toronto Star.*

Sanya Naqvi

GIDEON SALUTIN grew up in downtown Toronto without a religious upbringing or bar mitzvah. Instead, he learned the Bible's major stories through talks with his dad. In 2019, he founded the *Contemporary Review of Genocides* and interned with the United Nations. He attends McGill and carries a camera everywhere.

DUŠAN PETRIČIĆ is a Serbian illustrator and caricaturist who has lived in Canada for more than 20 years. He has illustrated numerous children's books and his cartoons and illustrations have appeared in various newspapers and magazines from *Politika* to *The New York Times*, the *Wall Street Journal*, *Scientific American*, and the *Toronto Star.*